Visual Fractions – A Beginning Fractions Book
Dr. Pi Squared

Nonfiction/children's/mathematics/arithmetic
Nonfiction/education/mathematics/arithmetic

ISBN-10: 1463542798. ISBN-13: 978-1463542795.

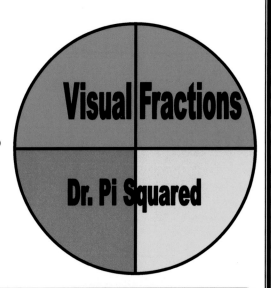

Introduction

This workbook provides practice determining fractions visually. For example, a circle may be divided into red, yellow, and blue pie slices, and the exercise may be to figure out what fraction of the slices are each color. Other shapes include triangles, squares, and hexagons; some exercises also feature smiley faces, letters, and numbers. The hope is that these exercises will help convey a sense of what fractions mean in a way that's easy to visualize.

Answers: Parents, teachers, or students may check the answers with the key at the back of the book. Note that the answers are all stated as reduced fractions.

Reduced fractions: Sometimes, a fraction may be written more than one way. For example, three-fourths of each pie below is colored blue. This shows that $\frac{9}{12}$ is equal to $\frac{3}{4}$; the form $\frac{3}{4}$ is called the reduced fraction, since it is simpler. If you divide the slices of the left pie into groups of three, you will see that three of the four groups are blue (and one group is yellow).

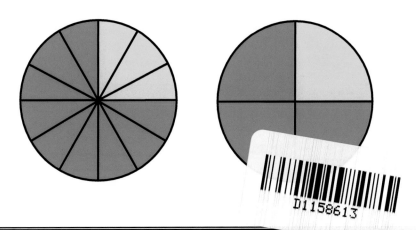

In each blank, write the fraction of the circle that is the given color.

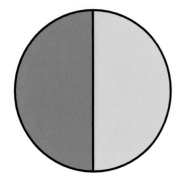
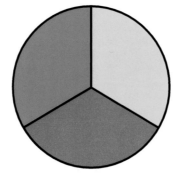
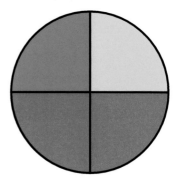

blue ___ $\frac{1}{2}$ ___

blue ___ $\frac{1}{3}$ ___

blue ___ $\frac{1}{4}$ ___

yellow ___ $\frac{1}{2}$ ___

yellow ___ $\frac{1}{3}$ ___

yellow ___ $\frac{1}{4}$ ___

red ___ $\frac{1}{3}$ ___

red ___ $\frac{1}{2}$ ___

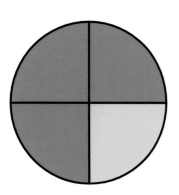
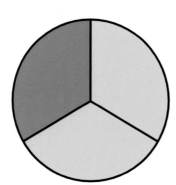
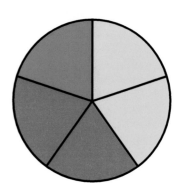

blue ___ $\frac{3}{4}$ ___

blue ___ $\frac{1}{3}$ ___

blue ___ $\frac{1}{5}$ ___

yellow ___ $\frac{1}{4}$ ___

yellow ___ $\frac{2}{3}$ ___

yellow ___ $\frac{3}{5}$ ___

red ___ $\frac{2}{5}$ ___

In each blank, write the fraction of the circle that is the given color.

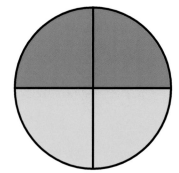

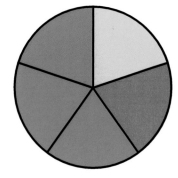

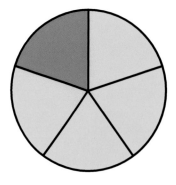

blue $\frac{1}{2}$ blue $\frac{3}{5}$ blue $\frac{1}{5}$

yellow $\frac{1}{2}$ yellow $\frac{1}{5}$ yellow $\frac{4}{5}$

red $\frac{1}{5}$

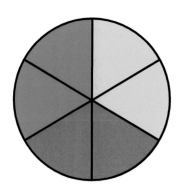

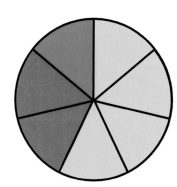

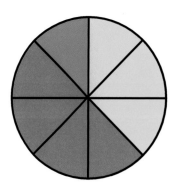

blue $\frac{2}{6}$ blue $\frac{1}{7}$ blue $\frac{1}{8}$

yellow $\frac{2}{6}$ yellow $\frac{4}{7}$ yellow $\frac{3}{8}$

red $\frac{2}{6} = \frac{1}{3}$ red $\frac{2}{7}$ red $\frac{1}{2}$

In each blank, write the fraction of the circle that is the given color.

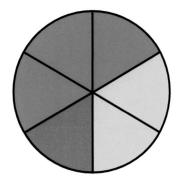

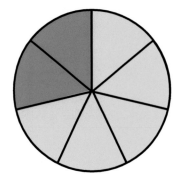

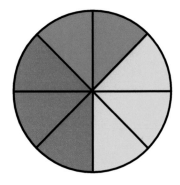

blue _____ $\frac{1}{2}$ _____

blue _____ $\frac{2}{7}$ _____

blue _____ $\frac{1}{4} = \frac{2}{8}$ _____

yellow _____ $\frac{2}{6} = \frac{1}{3}$ _____

yellow _____ $\frac{5}{7}$ _____

yellow _____ $\frac{3}{8}$ _____

red _____ $\frac{1}{6}$ _____

red _____ $\frac{3}{8}$ _____

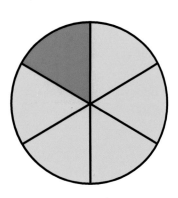

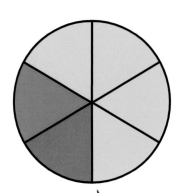

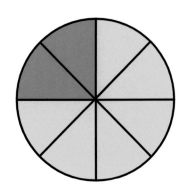

blue _____ $\frac{1}{6}$ _____

blue _____ $\frac{1}{6}$ _____

blue _____ $\frac{2}{8} = \frac{1}{4}$ _____

yellow _____ $\frac{5}{6}$ _____

yellow _____ $\frac{4-2}{6} \cdot \frac{1}{3}$ _____

yellow _____ $\frac{6}{8} = \frac{3}{4}$ _____

red _____ $\frac{1}{6}$ _____

In each blank, write the fraction of the circle that is the given color.

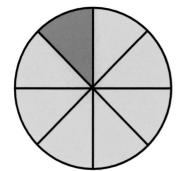
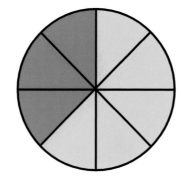
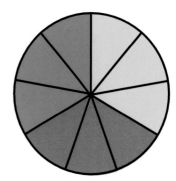

blue _____   blue _____   blue _____

yellow _____   yellow _____   yellow _____

                                                red _____

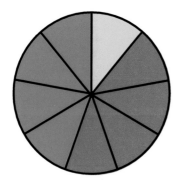
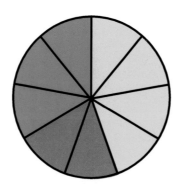
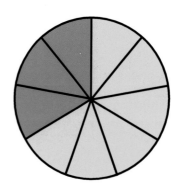

blue _____   blue _____   blue _____

yellow _____   yellow _____   yellow _____

red _____   red _____

In each blank, write the fraction of the circle that is the given color.

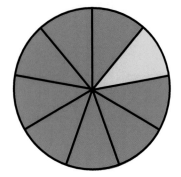

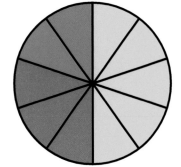

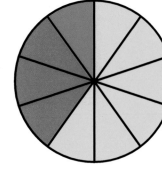

blue _____   blue _____   blue _____

yellow _____   yellow _____   yellow _____

                                       red _____   red _____

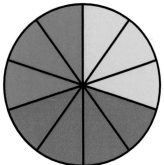

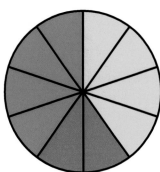

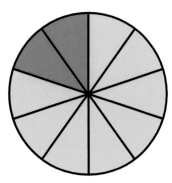

blue _____   blue _____   blue _____

yellow _____   yellow _____   yellow _____

red _____   red _____

In each blank, write the fraction of the circle that is the given color.

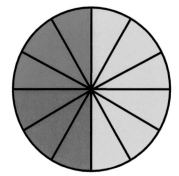 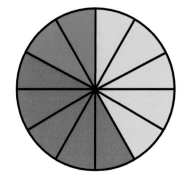 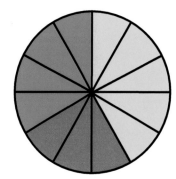

blue _____   blue _____   blue _____

yellow _____   yellow _____   yellow _____

red _____   red _____   red _____

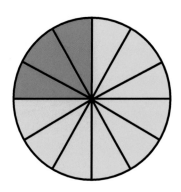 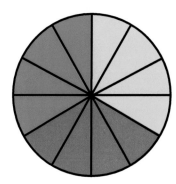 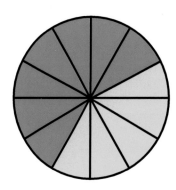

blue _____   blue _____   blue _____

yellow _____   yellow _____   yellow _____

red _____

In each blank, write the fraction of the circle that is the given color.

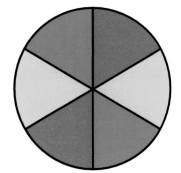 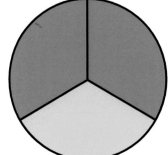 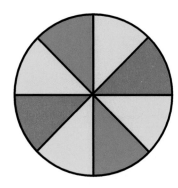

blue _____ blue _____ blue _____

yellow _____ yellow _____ yellow _____

red _____ red _____

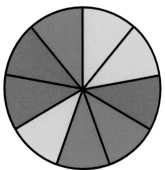  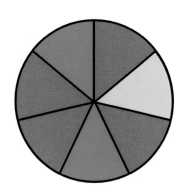

blue _____ blue _____ blue _____

yellow _____ yellow _____ yellow _____

red _____ red _____ red _____

In each blank, write the fraction of the circle that is the given color.

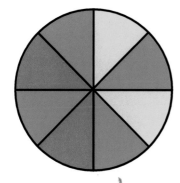

blue ___$\frac{1}{2}$___

yellow ___$\frac{2}{8}$___

red ___$\frac{2}{8}$___

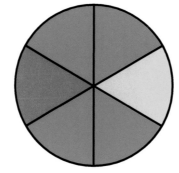

blue ___$\frac{4}{6}$___

yellow ___$\frac{1}{6}$___

red ___$\frac{1}{6}$___

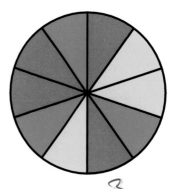

blue ___$\frac{3}{10}$___

yellow ___$\frac{3}{10}$___

red ___$\frac{4}{10}$___

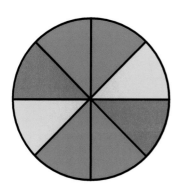

blue ___$\frac{1}{2}$___

yellow ___$\frac{2}{8}$___

red ___$\frac{2}{8}$___

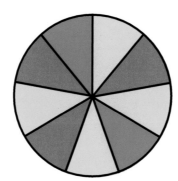

blue ___$\frac{2}{9}$___

yellow ___$\frac{4}{9}$___

red ___$\frac{3}{9}$___

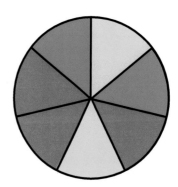

blue ___$\frac{2}{7}$___

yellow ___$\frac{2}{7}$___

red ___$\frac{3}{7}$___

In each blank, write the fraction of the triangle that is the given color.

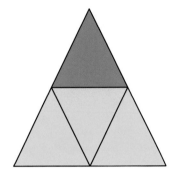

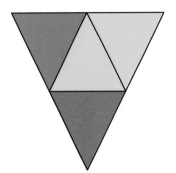

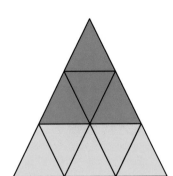

blue _____

blue _____

blue _____

yellow _____

yellow _____

yellow _____

red _____

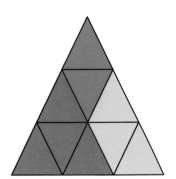

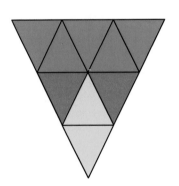

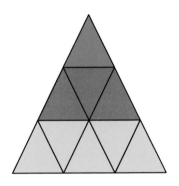

blue _____

blue _____

blue _____

yellow _____

yellow _____

yellow _____

red _____

red _____

red _____

In each blank, write the fraction of the triangle that is the given color.

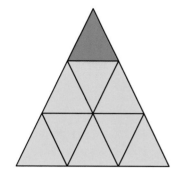

blue _____

yellow _____

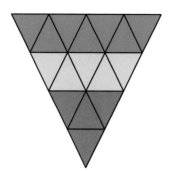

blue _____

yellow _____

red _____

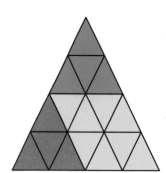

blue _____

yellow _____

red _____

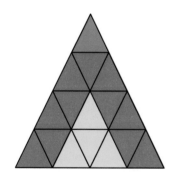

blue _____

yellow _____

red _____

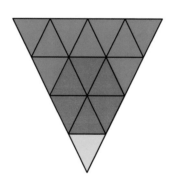

blue _____

yellow _____

red _____

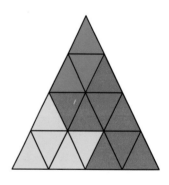

blue _____

yellow _____

red _____

In each blank, write the fraction of the triangle that is the given color.

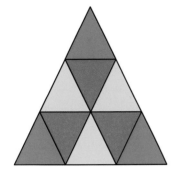

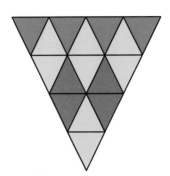

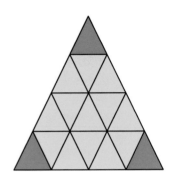

blue _____

yellow _____

red _____

blue _____

yellow _____

red _____

blue _____

yellow _____

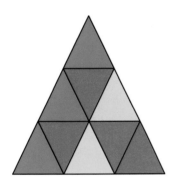

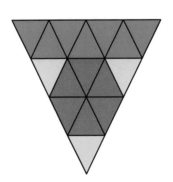

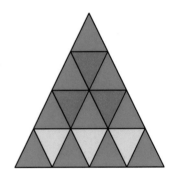

blue _____

yellow _____

red _____

blue _____

yellow _____

red _____

blue _____

yellow _____

red _____

In each blank, write the fraction of the square that is the given color.

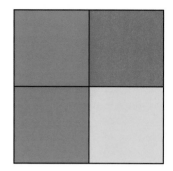

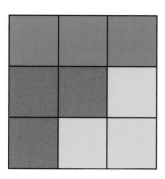

blue _____

yellow _____

red _____

blue _____

yellow _____

blue _____

yellow _____

red _____

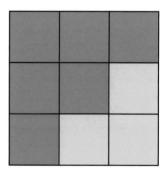

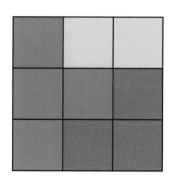

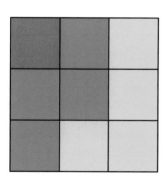

blue _____

yellow _____

blue _____

yellow _____

red _____

blue _____

yellow _____

red _____

In each blank, write the fraction of the square that is the given color.

blue _____

yellow _____

red _____

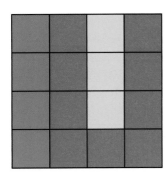

blue _____

yellow _____

red _____

blue _____

yellow _____

red _____

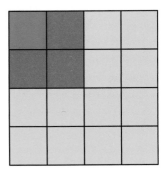

blue _____

yellow _____

red _____

blue _____

yellow _____

red _____

blue _____

yellow _____

red _____

In each blank, write the fraction of the square that is the given color.

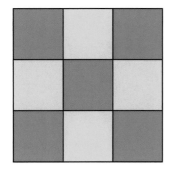

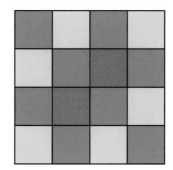

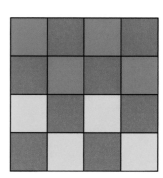

blue _____   blue _____   blue _____

yellow _____   yellow _____   yellow _____

                            red _____   red _____

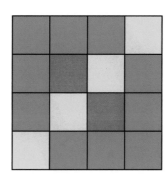

blue _____   blue _____   blue _____

yellow _____   yellow _____   yellow _____

red _____   red _____   red _____

In each blank, write the fraction of the hexagon that is the given color.

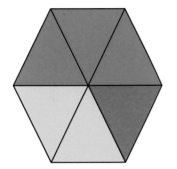 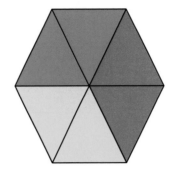 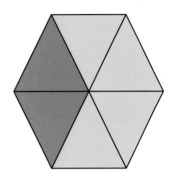

blue _____   blue _____   blue _____

yellow _____   yellow _____   yellow _____

red _____   red _____

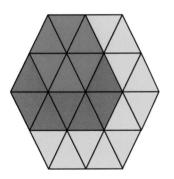 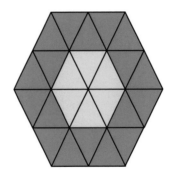

blue _____   blue _____   blue _____

yellow _____   yellow _____   yellow _____

red _____   red _____

16

In each blank, write the fraction of the hexagon that is the given color.

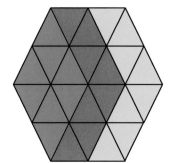 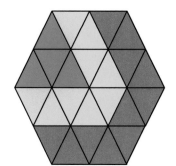 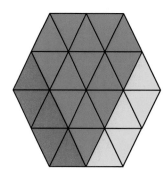

blue _____   blue _____   blue _____

yellow _____   yellow _____   yellow _____

red _____   red _____   red _____

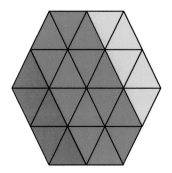 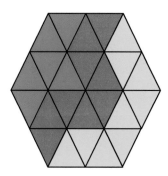 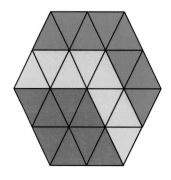

blue _____   blue _____   blue _____

yellow _____   yellow _____   yellow _____

red _____   red _____   red _____

In each blank, write the fraction of the hexagon that is the given color.

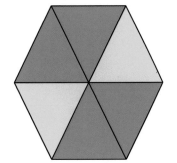

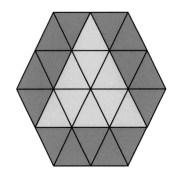

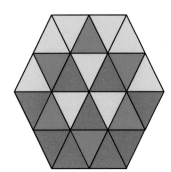

blue _____

yellow _____

blue _____

yellow _____

blue _____

yellow _____

red _____

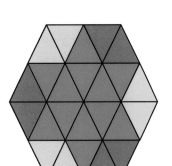

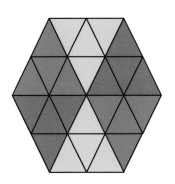

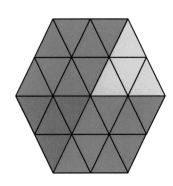

blue _____

yellow _____

red _____

blue _____

yellow _____

red _____

blue _____

yellow _____

red _____

Write a mixed number for your answer to these questions. For example, the mixed number $3\frac{1}{2}$ means three and one-half.

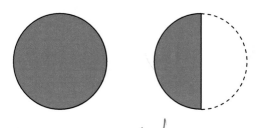

How many red circles are there? _____ $1\frac{1}{2}$ _____

How many blue circles are there? _____ $2\frac{1}{2}$ _____

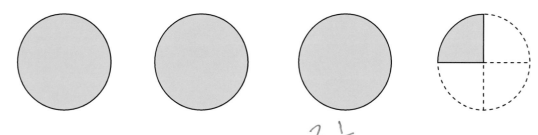

How many yellow circles are there? _____ $3\frac{1}{4}$ _____

How many green circles are there? _____ $2\frac{1}{3}$ _____

Write a mixed number for your answer to these questions. For example, the mixed number $3\frac{1}{2}$ means three and one-half.

How many red circles are there? _____ $2\frac{1}{4}$ _____

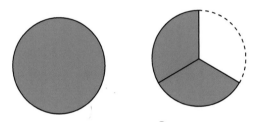

How many blue circles are there? _____ $1\frac{2}{3}$ _____

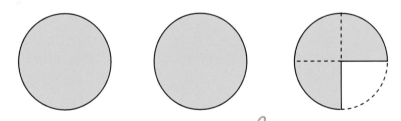

How many yellow circles are there? _____ $2\frac{3}{4}$ _____

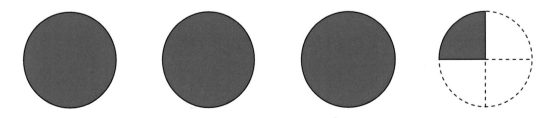

How many green circles are there? _____ $3\frac{1}{4}$ _____

In each blank, write the fraction of the rectangle that is the given color.

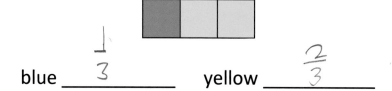

blue $\frac{1}{3}$ yellow $\frac{2}{3}$

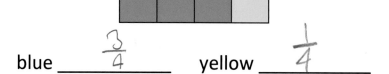

blue $\frac{3}{4}$ yellow $\frac{1}{4}$

blue $\frac{1}{5}$ yellow $\frac{1}{5}$ red $\frac{3}{5}$

blue $\frac{1}{2}$ yellow $\frac{1}{3}$ red $\frac{1}{6}$

blue $\frac{1}{2}$ yellow $\frac{1}{4}$ red $\frac{1}{4}$

blue $\frac{1}{6}$ yellow $\frac{4}{6} - \frac{2}{4}$ red $\frac{1}{6}$

In each blank, write the fraction of the rectangle that is the given color.

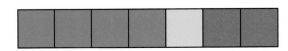

blue $\frac{4}{7}$ yellow $\frac{1}{7}$ red $\frac{2}{7}$

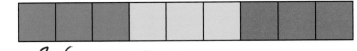

blue $\frac{1}{4} = \frac{2}{8}$ yellow $\frac{1}{2} = \frac{4}{8}$ red $\frac{2}{8} = \frac{1}{4}$

blue $\frac{1}{3} = \frac{3}{9} \cdot \frac{6}{12}$ yellow   red

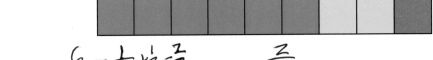

blue $\frac{3}{8}$ yellow $\frac{1}{4} = \frac{2}{8}$ red $\frac{5}{8}$

blue $\frac{6}{9} = \frac{1}{3} + \frac{1}{3} = \frac{2}{3}$ yellow $\frac{2}{9}$ red $\frac{1}{9}$

blue $\frac{2}{7}$ yellow $\frac{3}{7}$ red $\frac{2}{7}$

In each blank, write the fraction of the rectangle that is the given color.

blue _____   yellow _____   red _____

blue _____   yellow _____   red _____

blue _____   yellow _____   red _____

blue _____   yellow _____   red _____

blue _____   yellow _____   red _____

blue _____   yellow _____   red _____

In each blank, write the fraction of the rectangle that is the given color.

blue _____   yellow _____

blue _____   yellow _____   red _____

blue _____   yellow _____   red _____

blue _____   yellow _____   red _____

blue _____   yellow _____   red _____

blue _____   yellow _____   red _____

In each blank, write the fraction of the rectangle that is the given color.

blue _____   yellow _____

blue _____   yellow _____   red _____

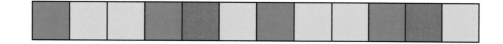

blue _____   yellow _____   red _____

blue _____   yellow _____   red _____

blue _____   yellow _____   red _____

blue _____   yellow _____   red _____

In each blank, write the fraction of the rectangle that is the given color.

blue _____   yellow _____

blue _____   yellow _____   red _____

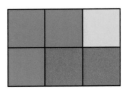

blue _____   yellow _____   red _____

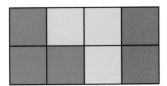

blue _____   yellow _____   red _____

In each blank, write the fraction of the rectangle that is the given color.

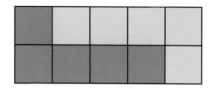

blue _____   yellow _____

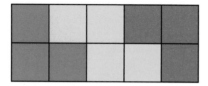

blue _____   yellow _____   red _____

blue _____   yellow _____   red _____

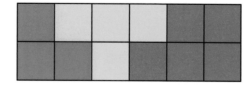

blue _____   yellow _____   red _____

In each blank, write the fraction of the rectangle that is the given color.

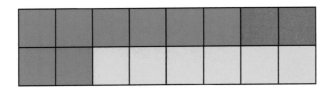

blue _____   yellow _____   red _____

blue _____   yellow _____   red _____

blue _____   yellow _____   red _____

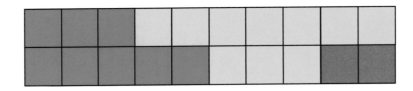

blue _____   yellow _____   red _____

In each blank, write the fraction of the rectangle that is the given color.

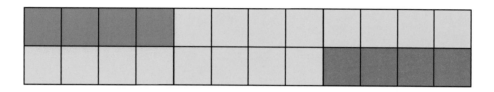

blue _____   yellow _____   red _____

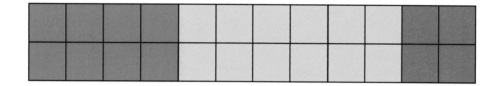

blue _____   yellow _____   red _____

blue _____   yellow _____   red _____

blue _____   yellow _____   red _____

In each blank, write the fraction of the rectangle that is the given color.

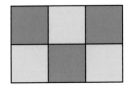

blue _____   yellow _____

blue _____   yellow _____   red _____

blue _____   yellow _____   red _____

blue _____   yellow _____   red _____

In each blank, write the fraction of the rectangle that is the given color.

blue _____   yellow _____   red _____

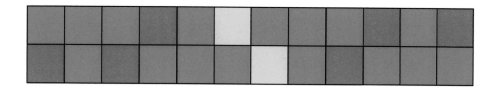

blue _____   yellow _____   red _____

blue _____   yellow _____   red _____

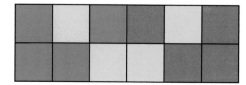

blue _____   yellow _____   red _____

In each blank, write the fraction of the faces that are the given color.

blue _____   yellow _____

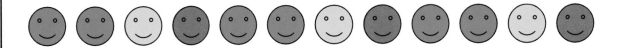

blue _____   yellow _____   red _____

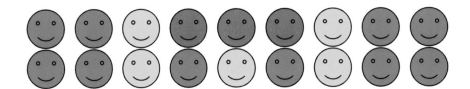

blue _____   yellow _____   red _____

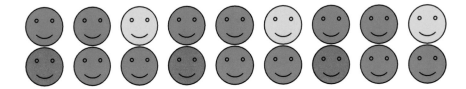

blue _____   yellow _____   red _____

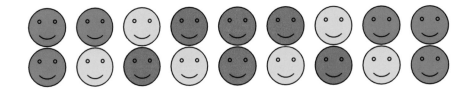

blue _____   yellow _____   red _____

What fraction are blue? _____ yellow? _____ circles? _____

triangles? _____ hexagons? _____ squares? _____

What fraction are yellow? _____ red? _____

up? _____ down? _____ right? _____ left? _____

What fraction are blue? _____ yellow? _____ red? _____

circles? _____ triangles? _____ squares? _____

What fraction are blue? _____ yellow? _____ red? _____

up? _____ down? _____ right? _____ left? _____

S C H O O L

What fraction are blue? _____ green? _____

red? _____ consonants? _____ vowels? _____

F R A C T I O N S

What fraction are blue? _____ green? _____

red? _____ consonants? _____ vowels? _____

A R I T H M E T I C

What fraction are blue? _____ green? _____

red? _____ consonants? _____ vowels? _____

M A T H E M A T I C S

What fraction are blue? _____ green? _____

red? _____ consonants? _____ vowels? _____

A b C d e F g H i j

What fraction are blue? _____ green? _____

red? _____ uppercase? _____ lowercase? _____

z Y X w V U t S R

What fraction are blue? _____ green? _____

red? _____ uppercase? _____ lowercase? _____

A c E G i K m O Q s

What fraction are blue? _____ green? _____

red? _____ uppercase? _____ lowercase? _____

Z X v T R p N L j

What fraction are blue? _____ green? _____

red? _____ uppercase? _____ lowercase? _____

Look at numbers, not digits. For example, 14 is a two-digit number.

1 , 2 , 3 , 4 , 5 , 6 , 7 , 8 , 9

What fraction are blue? _____ green? _____

red? _____ odd? _____ even? _____

2 , 4 , 6 , 8 , 10 , 12 , 14 , 16

What fraction are blue? _____ green? _____

red? _____ single-digit? _____ double-digit? _____

3 , 4 , 6 , 8 , 9 , 12 , 15 , 16

What fraction are blue? _____ red? _____

divisible by 3? _____ divisible by 4? _____ divisible by 6? _____

1 , 1 , 2 , 3 , 5 , 8 , 13 , 21

What fraction are blue? _____ green? _____

red? _____ odd? _____ even? _____

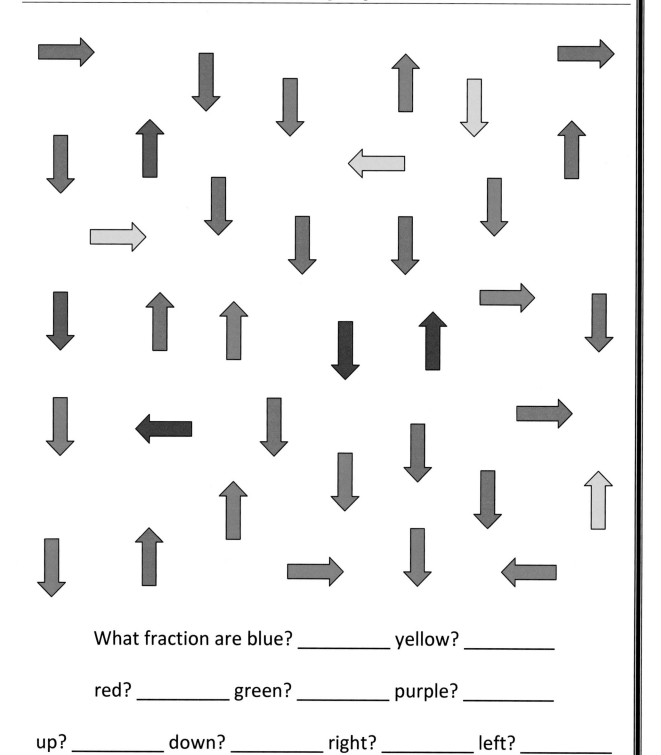

What fraction are blue? _____ yellow? _____

red? _____ green? _____ purple? _____

up? _____ down? _____ right? _____ left? _____

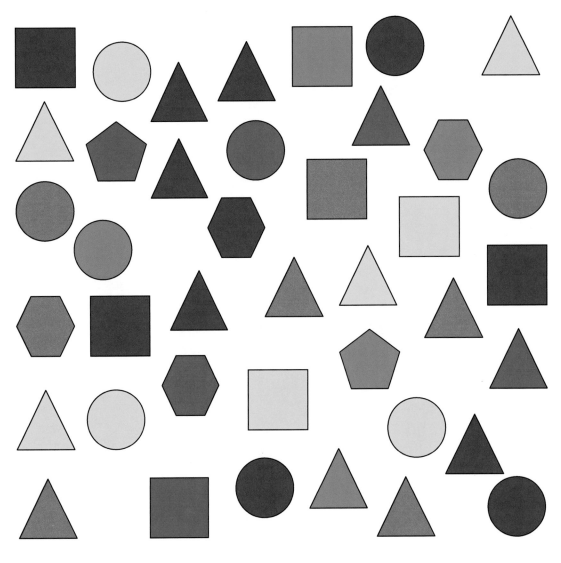

What fraction are blue? _____ yellow? _____

red? _____ green? _____ purple? _____

circles? _____ triangles? _____ squares? _____

pentagons? _____ hexagons? _____

What fraction of the shapes are blue? _____ yellow? _____

red? _____ green? _____ purple? _____

planets? _____ stars? _____

What fraction are blue? _____ yellow? _____

red? _____ green? _____ purple? _____

happy? _____ sad? _____

Answer Key

Note: Sometimes, there is more than one way to express the fraction. In this case, we have given the reduced fraction. For example, if 6 out of 9 circles are red, we could say that 6/9 are red. However, if 6 out of 9 are red, we can divide the circles into groups of 3, and see that 2 out of 3 of the groups are red, or that 2/3 of the circles are red. In this case, 2/3 is the reduced fraction; 2/3 is equal to 6/9. See page 1 for a visual example of this.

Page 2			Page 3			Page 4		
1/2	1/3	1/4	1/2	3/5	1/5	1/2	2/7	1/4
1/2	1/3	1/4	1/2	1/5	4/5	1/3	5/7	3/8
	1/3	1/2		1/5		1/6		3/8
3/4	1/3	1/5	1/3	1/7	1/8	1/6	1/6	1/4
1/4	2/3	2/5	1/3	4/7	3/8	5/6	2/3	3/4
		2/5	1/3	2/7	1/2		1/6	
Page 5			Page 6			Page 7		
1/8	3/8	1/3	8/9	1/5	1/10	1/4	1/6	1/3
7/8	5/8	1/3	1/9	1/2	3/5	1/2	5/12	5/12
		1/3		3/10	3/10	1/4	5/12	1/4
4/9	1/3	1/3	3/10	2/5	1/5	1/4	1/3	7/12
1/9	4/9	2/3	3/10	2/5	4/5	3/4	1/3	5/12
4/9	2/9		2/5	1/5			1/3	
Page 8			Page 9			Page 10		
1/3	2/3	1/4	1/2	2/3	3/10	1/4	1/4	4/9
1/3	1/3	1/2	1/4	1/6	3/10	3/4	1/2	5/9
1/3		1/4	1/4	1/6	2/5		1/4	
1/3	1/2	2/7	1/2	2/9	2/7	2/9	5/9	1/9
1/3	1/4	1/7	1/4	4/9	2/7	1/3	2/9	5/9
1/3	1/4	4/7	1/4	1/3	3/7	4/9	2/9	1/3

Page 11			Page 12			Page 13		
1/9	7/16	1/4	1/3	1/4	3/16	1/2	3/4	1/3
8/9	5/16	1/2	1/3	1/2	13/16	1/4	1/4	1/3
	1/4	1/4	1/3	1/4		1/4		1/3
1/16	9/16	3/16	1/3	7/16	5/8	2/3	4/9	4/9
1/4	1/16	5/16	2/9	3/16	3/16	1/3	2/9	4/9
11/16	3/8	1/2	4/9	3/8	3/16		1/3	1/9

Page 14			Page 15			Page 16		
1/9	1/4	1/4	5/9	1/2	1/4	1/2	1/3	1/3
2/3	1/2	3/16	4/9	3/8	1/4	1/3	1/3	2/3
2/9	1/4	9/16		1/8	1/2	1/6	1/3	
1/16	7/16	3/8	1/4	5/8	3/8	1/4	3/4	5/24
3/4	5/16	3/8	1/2	1/4	1/4	11/24	1/4	7/24
3/16	1/4	1/4	1/4	1/8	3/8	7/24		1/2

Page 17			Page 18			Page 19
1/3	1/6	7/12	2/3	5/8	1/4	$1\frac{1}{2}$
1/3	3/8	5/24	1/3	3/8	3/8	$2\frac{1}{2}$
1/3	11/24	5/24			3/8	$3\frac{1}{4}$
7/12	1/4	1/3	1/2	1/3	2/3	$2\frac{1}{3}$
5/24	3/8	1/3	1/4	1/3	1/6	
5/24	3/8	1/3	1/4	1/3	1/6	

Page 20	Page 21			Page 22		
$2\frac{1}{4}$	1/3	2/3		4/7	1/7	2/7
$1\frac{2}{3}$	3/4	1/4		1/4	1/2	1/4
$2\frac{3}{4}$	1/5	1/5	3/5	1/3	1/3	1/3
$3\frac{1}{4}$	1/2	1/3	1/6	3/8	1/4	3/8
	1/2	1/4	1/4	2/3	2/9	1/9
	1/6	2/3	1/6	2/7	3/7	2/7

Page 23			Page 24			Page 25		
1/2	3/10	1/5	4/7	3/7		4/5	1/5	
1/10	1/2	2/5	1/2	1/4	1/4	1/5	1/2	3/10
1/6	2/3	1/6	1/3	1/3	1/3	1/3	1/2	1/6
1/5	2/5	2/5	1/2	1/4	1/4	2/5	3/10	3/10
1/3	1/3	1/3	2/9	4/9	1/3	1/2	1/3	1/6
1/4	1/2	1/4	3/7	2/7	2/7	1/2	1/3	1/6

Page 26			Page 27			Page 28		
2/3	1/3		1/2	1/2		1/2	3/8	1/8
1/2	3/8	1/8	3/10	2/5	3/10	1/2	1/4	1/4
1/2	1/6	1/3	1/2	1/3	1/6	1/4	1/2	1/4
3/8	3/8	1/4	1/4	1/3	5/12	2/5	1/2	1/10

Page 29			Page 30			Page 31		
1/6	2/3	1/6	1/2	1/2		1/2	3/10	1/5
1/3	1/2	1/6	1/4	1/2	1/4	1/2	3/8	1/8
3/14	2/7	1/2	1/5	3/5	1/5	1/3	1/3	1/3
9/28	3/7	1/4	3/8	1/2	1/8	2/3	1/12	1/4

Page 32

2/3	1/3	
1/2	1/4	1/4
5/9	5/18	1/6
2/3	1/6	1/6
1/3	1/3	1/3

Page 33

1/4	3/4	1/8	
1/2	1/8	1/4	
2/3	1/3		
1/6	1/3	1/3	1/6
1/3	1/3	1/3	
1/2	1/6	1/3	
1/3	1/2	1/6	
1/2	1/6	1/6	1/6

Page 34

1/3	1/2	
1/6	2/3	1/3
1/3	2/9	
4/9	2/3	1/3
1/5	3/5	
1/5	3/5	2/5
3/11	4/11	
4/11	7/11	4/11

Page 35

2/5	1/5	
2/5	2/5	3/5
5/9	2/9	
2/9	2/3	1/3
1/5	1/5	
3/5	3/5	2/5
4/9	2/9	
1/3	2/3	1/3

Page 36

5/9	2/9	
2/9	5/9	4/9
1/8	3/4	
1/8	1/2	1/2
1/4	3/4	
5/8	1/2	1/4
1/4	1/2	
1/4	3/4	1/4

Page 37

1/3	1/9		
5/12	1/18	1/12	
1/4	1/2	1/6	1/12

Page 38

1/8	9/40	
1/5	3/20	3/10
1/4	2/5	1/5
1/20	1/10	

Page 39

2/5	1/5	
1/5	3/25	2/25
3/5	2/5	

Page 40

1/3	1/8	
1/4	1/8	1/6
2/3	1/3	

Made in the USA
Monee, IL
13 December 2020